Baby Record Book

p

 What's to come...

The First Nine Months

Family Tree

My Birth

My Appearance

First Days

Coming Home

My Name

The Announcement

Hands, Feet, Hair, Teeth!

Growing Chart

First Sounds

First Steps

Special 'Firsts'

My Likes and Dislikes

Bath and Bedtime

My Health

My First Christmas

First Holidays

My First Birthday

Favourite Things

Special Memories

The First Nine Months

It takes nine months to grow a baby - that's a long time
to wait for something really exciting to happen!

Mummy and Daddy first found out I was coming on: . . . .

Their first reaction was: (Mummy) . . . .

. . . .

(Daddy) . . . .

. . . .

They first heard my heartbeat on: . . . .

. . . .

Mummy first felt me kicking on: . . . .

Whilst she was pregnant with me, Mummy had some strange food
cravings. Here are some of them: . . . .

. . . .

. . . .

Here is a picture of my first scan. It doesn't look much like me –
just wait until I start growing!

Photo

This scan was taken on:. . . . .

Ride a Cock Horse

Ride a cock horse to Banbury Cross
To see a fine lady ride on a white horse
Rings on her fingers and bells on her toes
She shall have music wherever she goes!

 # Family Tree

Families are like apple trees - they grow branches and yield lots of fruit!

This is the family I was born into.

Parents

Father's Parents

Mother's Parents

Parents

Brothers/Sisters

Brothers

Baby

Sisters

Grandparents

Mummy's name is:

. . . .

She was born on:

. . . .

Daddy's name is:

. . . .

He was born on:

. . . .

Mummy and Daddy first met on:

. . . .

Other family members are:. . . . .

. . . .

. . . .

Mary Mary Quite Contrary

Mary Mary quite contrary
How does your garden grow?
With cockle shells and silver bells
And pretty maids all in a row.

 **My Birth**

All good things come to those who wait - and at last I arrived, the latest rosy apple on the family tree!

I was expected on:

Day. . . . . Date. . . . . Month. . . . . Year. . . . .

I arrived on:

Day. . . . . Date. . . . . Month. . . . . Year. . . . .

I was born at: . . . .

Monday's Child

Monday's child is fair of face

Tuesday's child is full of grace

Wednesday's child is full of woe

Thursday's child has far to go

Friday's child is loving and giving

Saturday's child works hard for a living

But the child that is born on the Sabbath day

Is happy and bright in every way.

These are the people who helped Mummy at my birth:

. . . .

. . . .

. . . .

. . . .

. . . .

Hey Diddle Diddle

Hey diddle diddle, the cat and the fiddle
The cow jumped over the moon
The little dog laughed to see such fun
And the dish ran away with the spoon!

Photo

My Appearance

Newborn babies don't look like anything except - newborn babies! But after a while they start to resemble other people in the family.

Bye Baby Bunting

Bye baby bunting
Daddy's gone a-hunting!
To fetch a little rabbit skin
To wrap the baby bunting in.

This is how I looked when I was born:

Eyes: . . . .

Hair: . . . .

Weight: . . . .

Length: . . . .

These are the changes that took place in my appearance over the first few weeks of my life:. . . . .

. . . .

. . . .

Mummy says I look like: . . . .

Daddy says I look like: . . . .

Other people say I look like: . . . .

Here's a photograph of me at. . . . . weeks old.

I think I look just like me!

Photo

I Am Me

I am me

Who else could I be?

Babies do a lot of sleeping in their first few days and I was no exception!

These are some of the other things I did:

....

....

....

....

Lots of people were curious to see me. Some of my first visitors

were:. . . . .

....

....

....

Rock-a-Bye Baby

Rock-a-bye baby in the treetops

When the wind blows, the cradle will rock

When the bough breaks, the cradle will fall

Down will come baby, cradle and all.

Mummy and I got lots of cards and presents.

Here are a few of them:

. . . . from. . . . .

. . . . from. . . . .

. . . . from. . . . .

. . . . from. . . . .

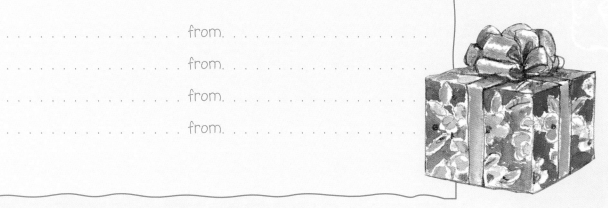

Hush Little Baby

Hush little baby, don't say a word
Daddy's going to buy you a mocking bird
If that mocking bird don't sing
Daddy's going to buy you a diamond ring
If that diamond ring is glass
Daddy's going to buy you a looking glass
If that looking glass gets broke
Daddy's going to buy you a billy goat
If that billy goat runs away
Tara tara boom-di-ay!

Home is where the heart is, and I was glad to arrive safely
at my home!

Mummy and Daddy brought me home for the first time on: . . . .

. . . .

My new home is: . . . .

. . . .

My family has lived here for: . . . .

These are the people that live in my home: . . . .

. . . .

These are the people that were waiting to greet me when I first arrived

home: . . . .

. . . .

. . . .

. . . .

On my first night home, I fell asleep
at: . . . .

. . . .

and woke up at: . . . .

. . . .

East, West

East, west
Home's best.

My Name

Some babies are named after their Mummy and Daddy or their grandparents. Others are named after friends. However it happens - a name is for life, so it's important to get it right!

These are some of the names that Mummy and Daddy thought of calling me:

If I were a girl: . . . .

If I were a boy: . . . .

But in the end they called me: . . . .

because: . . . .

My nickname is: . . . .

because: . . . .

My Christening or Naming Day celebration was on: . . . .

at: . . . .

My godparents are: . . . .

. . . .

. . . .

Here's a photograph of me on my special day!

Photo

Elizabeth, Elspeth, Betsey and Bess

Elizabeth, Elspeth, Betsey and Bess,
They all went together to seek a bird's nest
They found a bird's nest with five eggs in
They all took one, and left four in.

The Announcement

Everybody likes to hear that a new baby has arrived safely!

My birth was announced in the following way:. . . . .

. . . .

These are the words Mummy and Daddy used to announce my

arrival:. . . . .

. . . .

. . . .

Because I was born in the month of:. . . . .

my star sign is: . . . .

These are some of the characteristics of my star sign:. . . . .

. . . .

. . . .

. . . .

And here are some of my own early characteristics!. . . . .

. . . .

. . . .

Hark! Hark! the Dogs do Bark

Hark! Hark! The dogs do bark

The beggars are coming to town

Some in rags

And some in tags

And one in a velvet gown!

Hands, Feet, Hair, Teeth!

Here are outlines of my hands and feet that
Mummy and Daddy drew when I
was. . . . . months old!

Here's my hand. . .

. . . here's my foot. . .

. . . . and here's a lock of my hair!

I began teething on: . . . .

My first tooth appeared on: . . . .

My second tooth appeared on: . . . .

My third tooth appeared on: . . . .

My fourth tooth appeared on: . . . .

My fifth tooth appeared on: . . . .

I had a full set of teeth on: . . . .

Curly Locks, Curly Locks

Curly Locks, Curly Locks will you be mine?

You shall not wash dishes, nor yet feed the swine

But sit on a cushion and sew a fine seam

And dine upon strawberries, sugar and cream.

Growing Chart

Like a little seedling, I soon started to sprout upwards! This chart shows my progress.

	DATE	HEIGHT	WEIGHT
I am now 3 months:			
I am now 6 months:			
I am now 9 months:			
I am now 12 months:			
I am now 18 months:			
I am now 36 months:			

Here is a photograph to show how much I changed!

Photo

Girls and Boys Come Out to Play

Girls and boys come out to play
The moon doth shine as bright as day
Come with a whoop and come with a call
Come with a good will or not at all!

In the beginning I couldn't say much, but I liked to say it LOUDLY! Soon I learned which sounds produced food and which made everyone smile.

The first sounds I made were: . . . .

The first word I ever said was: . . . . on: . . . .

I first laughed on: . . . .

at (e.g. Mummy/Daddy/a song): . . . .

I first said 'Mummy' on: . . . .

I first said 'Daddy' on: . . . .

I spoke my first complete sentence on: . . . .

This is what I said: . . . .

. . . .

This is how everyone reacted: . . . .

. . . .

. . . .

One, Two, Buckle my Shoe

One, two, buckle my shoe
Three, four, knock on the door
Five, six, pick up sticks
Seven, eight, open the gate
Nine, ten, start again!

 **First Steps**

It wasn't long before I discovered that the world was an interesting place,
with lots to see and TOUCH!

I first held my head up on:. . . . .

I first clapped my hands on:. . . . .

I first rolled right over on:. . . . .

I first started to crawl on:. . . . .

I first sat up on:. . . . .

I first started pulling myself to my feet on:. . . . .

And I took my first steps on:. . . . .

when I was:. . . . . months old. I was walking

towards:. . . . . and everyone thought I was very clever!

Dr Foster Went to Gloucester

Dr Foster went to Gloucester
In a shower of rain
Stepped in a puddle right up to his middle
And never went there again!

Round and Round the Garden

Round and round the garden
Like a teddy bear
One step, two steps
Tickly under there!

Special 'Firsts'

Everything was new and exciting to me. This page is a record of some of the 'firsts' I experienced in the first year of my life.

First smile:

Date: . . . . .Details:. . . . .

. . . .

First day out:

Date: . . . . .Details:. . . . .

. . . .

First babysitter:

Date: . . . . .Details:. . . . .

. . . .

First ate solid food:

Date: . . . . .Details:. . . . .

. . . .

First ate with a spoon:

Date: . . . . .Details:. . . . .

. . . .

First haircut:

Date: . . . . .Details:. . . . .

. . . .

First friends:

Date:. . . . . Details:. . . . .

. . . .

First saw snow:

Date:. . . . . Details:. . . . .

. . . .

Other firsts:

Date:. . . . . Details:. . . . .

. . . .

Date:. . . . . Details:. . . . .

. . . .

Date:. . . . . Details:. . . . .

. . . .

My Likes and Dislikes

Some things made me laugh! Other things made me cry. These are some
of my early likes and dislikes, with particular attention to the most
important thing of all - FOOD!

I liked: . . . .

But I didn't like: . . . .

I liked: . . . .

But I didn't like: . . . .

I liked: . . . .

But I didn't like: . . . .

I liked: . . . .

But I didn't like: . . . .

I especially LOVED: . . . .

And I especially DIDN'T LIKE: . . . .

Jack Sprat

Jack Sprat would eat no fat, his wife would eat no lean
And so between the two of them, they licked the platter clean!

Pease Pudding Hot

Pease pudding hot, pease pudding cold
Pease pudding in the pot, nine days old!

 # Bath and Bedtime

Mummy and Daddy soon discovered that I did/did not like to be bathed.

This is their description of me in the bath:

. . . .

. . . .

I had my first bath at home on:. . . . .

My favourite bath toys are:. . . . .

. . . .

Rub-a-Dub-Dub,

Rub-a-dub-dub, three men in a tub
And how do you think they got there?
The butcher, the baker, the candlestick-maker
They all jumped out of a rotten potato!
'Twas enough to make a fish stare.

The Man in the Moon

The man in the moon
Looked out of the moon
And this is what he said:
'Tis time that, now I'm getting up,
All babies went to bed!

I first slept in a cot on: . . . .

My favourite bedtime toys are: . . . .

My favourite bedtime teddy is: . . . .

My favourite lullabies are: . . . .

I first slept through the night on: . . . .

Mummy and Daddy were very happy!

Here's a picture of me in pyjamas!:

Photo

My Health

It's surprising how many injections and tests a poor little baby needs! And how many coughs, colds and splutters a child can catch. Here is a medical history of my first year.

Injections:

Date: My age: Details:

. . . .

Date: My age: Details:

. . . .

Date: My age: Details:

. . . .

Eye tests:

Date: My age: Details:

. . . .

Date: My age: Details:

. . . .

Hearing tests:

Date: My age: Details:

. . . .

Date: My age: Details:

. . . .

Illnesses:

Date: . . . . My age: . . . . Details: . . . .

Date: . . . . My age: . . . . Details: . . . .

Date: . . . . My age: . . . . Details: . . . .

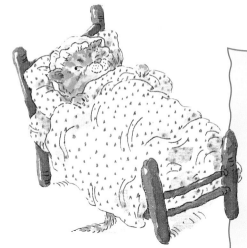

I am allergic to the following:. . . . .

. . . .

The doctor who looked after me was called:. . . . .

Early to Bed

Early to bed and early to rise
Makes a man healthy, wealthy and wise.

My First Christmas

My first Christmas was a special occasion. The house was
decorated with lights and tinsel, and everyone
gave me presents!

Here are some details of my first Christmas:

We spent Christmas at: . . . .

This is who came: . . . .

This is what we ate: . . . .

These are some of my presents:

. . . . from. . . . .

. . . . from. . . . .

. . . . from. . . . .

. . . . from. . . . .

The Holly and the Ivy

The holly and the ivy
When they are both full grown
Of all the trees that are in the wood
The holly bears the crown.

My first New Year celebration was spent at: . . . .

with: . . . .

. . . .

. . . .

. . . .

Christmas is Coming

Christmas is coming, the goose is getting fat

Please put a penny in the old man's hat

If you haven't got a penny, a ha'penny will do

If you haven't got a ha'penny ⁊ God bless you!

First Holidays

Mummy and Daddy took me on lots of trips and holidays when I was little. I soon discovered what an enormous and interesting world we live in!

We went to:. . . . . on: . . . .

We went with:. . . . .

We travelled by:. . . . .

We stayed at:. . . . .

My favourite activity was:. . . . .

My favourite outings were:. . . . .

. . . .

. . . .

. . . .

. . . .

Here is a photograph of me on my holiday!

Photo

The World

The world is so full of a number of things
I'm sure we should all be happy as kings!

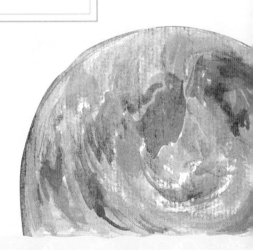

My First Birthday

And suddenly I was one year old - didn't time fly! Now I can walk and talk and do lots of interesting things!

We celebrated my first birthday with (e.g. a party, a special dinner):

....

I wore: . . . .

These are the people that helped me to celebrate: . . . .

. . . .

This is what we ate: . . . .

. . . .

These are some of my presents:

. . . . from. . . . .

. . . . from. . . . .

. . . . from. . . . .

. . . . from. . . . .

And here's a picture of me blowing out the candle on my cake!

Photo

Favourite Things

It didn't take long to discover which things I liked better than anything else in the world! Here are a few of them.

My favourite nursery rhyme: . . . .

My favourite toys: . . . .

My favourite game: . . . .

My favourite picture: . . . .

My favourite book: . . . .

My favourite people: . . . .

My favourite television programme: . . . .

My favourite animal: . . . .

Things that made me laugh: . . . .

Of course not everything made me happy! Some of the things I didn't like were: . . . .

. . . .

. . . .

. . . .

The Grand Old Duke of York

Oh the Grand Old Duke of York
He had ten thousand men
He marched them up to the top of the hill
And he marched them down again!
And when they were up, they were up
And when they were down, they were down
And when they were only half-way up
They were neither up nor down!

Oranges and Lemons

"Oranges and lemons," say the bells of St. Clements
"You owe me five farthings," say the bells of St. Martins
"When will you pay me?" say the bells of Old Bailey
"When I get rich," say the bells of Shoreditch
"When will that be?" say the bells of Old Clee
"I do not know," say the great bells of Bow
Here comes a candle to light you to bed
And here comes a chopper to chop off your head!

Special Memories

My early months are full of special memories.

Visits

My first big visit was a very special occasion that took lots of planning!
Here are some of the details of who we visited, who came with us, who
was there, what I wore and how I behaved!

....

....

Other memorable visits were:

....

....

....

Baa Baa Black Sheep

Baa baa black sheep, have you any wool?
Yes sir, yes sir, three bags full
One for the master, one for the dame
And one for the little child that lives down the lane.

Special moments

Every moment of a baby's life is precious, but here are a few particularly
memorable ones that Mummy and Daddy will never forget:

. . . .

. . . .

. . . .

The future

Mummy and Daddy have lots of special plans and hopes for my future.
Here are a few of them:

. . . .

. . . .

. . . .

. . . .

I Love Little Pussy

I love little pussy, her coat is so warm
And if I don't hurt her, she'll do me no harm
So I'll not pull her tail, nor drive her away
But pussy and I very gently will play.

Here are some photos of me during my first year:

Photographs